The *Believer's* Authority

Mission: To Proclaim Transformation and Truth

Published by: Transformed Publishing
Website: www.transformedpublishing.com
Email: transformedpublishing@gmail.com

Copyright © 2020 by Diana Robinson

All rights reserved solely by the author. No part of this book may be reproduced, stored in a retrieval system, or transmitted in any form or by any means without expressed written permission of the author.

Cover Image & Illustration (pg. 8) Created by Timeless Photography Plus, Antonio Collins

Exerts from *The Robe of Many Colors*, by Diana Robinson
Copyright © 2019 by Diana Robinson
Publisher Trilogy Christian Publishing
Available at www.transformedpublishing.com/book-store

Unless otherwise noted:
Scriptures are taken from the New King James Version ®. Copyright © 1982 by Thomas Nelson. Used by permission. All rights reserved.

As noted:
Scriptures are taken from The Message Version Copyright © 1993, 2002, 2018 by Eugene H. Peterson

The *Believer's* Authority

How to Overcome Bible Study Series

Study Guide, Workbook, & Journal

by Diana Robinson

Table of Contents

Introduction:	The Importance of Mind Transformation	1
Session 1:	The Believer	3
Session 2:	The Authorization	5
Session 3:	The Authority	7
Session 4:	The Power	9
Session 5:	The Planting	11
Session 6:	The Fruition	13
Journal Pages:	w/ Inspirational Scriptures	16

Directions:

This Study Guide, Workbook, & Journal is broken down into six sessions. It is recommended that you spend an entire week of devotional time studying, meditating, praying, and journaling on each topic. Additional journaling pages are located in the back of this book.

The Word of God is meant to cleanse, transform, refresh, & renew our minds. Mind transformation is a continuous process that we must do diligently. Ultimately, we must 'lose our mind' and *let* the mind of Christ root and take dominion in our mind.

Hebrews 9:14

[H]ow much more shall the blood of Christ, who through the eternal Spirit offered Himself without spot to God, cleanse your conscience from dead works to serve the living God?

Philippians 2:5-11

Let this mind be in you which was also in Christ Jesus, [6] who, being in the form of God, did not consider it robbery to be equal with God, [7] but made Himself of no reputation, taking the form of a bondservant, and coming in the likeness of men. [8] And being found in appearance as a man, He humbled Himself and became obedient to *the point of* death, even the death of the cross. [9] Therefore God also has highly exalted Him and given Him the name which is above every name, [10] that at the name of Jesus every knee should bow, of those in heaven, and of those on earth, and of those under the earth, [11] and *that* every tongue should confess that Jesus Christ *is* Lord, to the glory of God the Father.

Introduction
The Importance of Mind Transformation

Mind transformation is the greatest miracle that has taken place in my life. The power to void plaguing destructive thinking patterns is readily available. Application of the principles found in God's Word is essential and they work for those who work them!

> I beseech you therefore, brethren, by the mercies of God, that you present your bodies a living sacrifice, holy, acceptable to God, *which* is your reasonable service. And do not be conformed to this world, but be transformed by the renewing of your mind, that you may prove what is that good and acceptable and perfect will of God.
>
> Romans 12:1-2

> Who remembered us in our lowly state, For His mercy *endures* forever; And rescued us from our enemies, For His mercy *endures* forever; Who gives food to all flesh, For His mercy *endures* forever. Oh, give thanks to the God of heaven! For His mercy *endures* forever.
>
> Psalm 136:23-26

To beseech is to cry out with great desire for someone to hear and benefit from the words coming next. When we were caught up in the very act of the worst things we have ever done, it was God who saw past that moment of time, *our lowly state*, and extended His mercy unto us. In honor of His mercy, choose to present your body, mind, and spirit as a living sacrifice; holy and acceptable to God. *Conformed* means to take the shape of the surroundings, as liquid does when it is poured from container to container. You are called to be *transformed* by the renewing of your mind. The transformed mind is a weapon of warfare that makes you, "steadfast, immovable, always abounding in the work of the Lord, knowing that your labor is not in vain in the Lord" (1 Corinthians 15:58). Christ desires your mind to be identifiably transformed for your sake and for His. In the doing of the work of the Word, you prove what is *that* good, acceptable, and perfect will of God.

Combining the many people, influences, and life experiences that mold our minds with spiritual fiery darts of the wicked one, no wonder people are desperately seeking mind alteration. All these factors, however, are not responsible for the corruption of the mind. What we allow to breed in the inner man leads to defilement. Jesus taught in Mark 7:15, "There is nothing that enters a man from outside which can defile him; but the things which come out of him, those are the things that defile a man." Output is created by thoughts meditated on, that become feelings, then behavior.

*Exert from *The Robe of Many Colors,* by Diana Robinson

Love,

Diana Robinson

Get More Christian Books by Transformed Publishing Authors at www.transformedpublishing.com/book-store
EMAIL DIRECTLY for bulk order pricing:
transformedpublishing@gmail.com

◆ *The Robe of Many Colors: Obedience Overcomes Obstacles*, by Diana Robinson

Do you need a resource to help combat anxiety, disappointment, discouragement, temptation, distraction, inferiority, & oppression? This book will awaken the vision within you to operate confidently in all God has entrusted and equipped you with. Proven principles from the life of Joseph are the framework for each chapter. Discover the benefits of obedience.

◆ *Exploring The Fruits of The Spirit with Joy*, by Diana Robinson

Relevant and engaging for children of all ages. Use this book to teach, empower, and talk to your children about making Jesus' PEACE a reality by choosing to be full of joy and love, even when things do not go their way.

◆ *My Story: How God Delivered, Healed, & Set Me Free*, by Tawnya J. Jackson

This book is for single parents, people in questionable relationships, and those who are tired of being sick & tired! Tawnya honestly shares her heart and transition from despair and hopelessness to deliverance, healing, and freedom. My Story is full of strength, inspiration, and wisdom.

◆ *A Glimpse Into My Heart: Poems of Inspiration,* by Babette Bailey

This collection of poems was sparked by many different people, events, hopes, dreams, issues, and a lot of other things that have touched & impacted Babette's heart in different ways. Just like our lives, like a good song, or like a fresh new idea that could go on and on in our minds, these glimpses are meant to open the heart, gently lift the heart, and bring a spark to the heart that will go on and on.

◆ *From Servants to Sons*, by Diana Hicks

Moving from servitude to Sonship brings forth authority and an inheritance. It brings the Spirit of the Holy Ghost which affords us the opportunity to be in the family of God. Remember if we are led by God, we have been given power to become Sons. This is not the time to give up but to push and to establish a real relationship with God. It is time to seek the Lord. To partake of this next season, we must become Sons of God. Get this book and discover your covenant rights as Sons of God.

Session 1: The Believer

Romans 8:8-13

But what does it say? "The word is near you, in your mouth and in your heart" (that is, the word of faith which we preach): ⁹ that if you confess with your mouth the Lord Jesus and believe in your heart that God has raised Him from the dead, you will be saved. ¹⁰ For with the heart one believes unto righteousness, and with the mouth confession is made unto salvation. ¹¹ For the Scripture says, "Whoever believes on Him will not be put to shame." ¹² For there is no distinction between Jew and Greek, for the same Lord over all is rich to all who call upon Him. ¹³ For "whoever calls on the name of the LORD shall be saved."

John 3:2-3

This man [Nicodemus] came to Jesus by night and said to Him, "Rabbi, we know that You are a teacher come from God; for no one can do these signs that You do unless God is with him." ³ Jesus answered and said to him, "Most assuredly, I say to you, unless one is born again, he cannot see the kingdom of God."

John 3:14-21

And as Moses lifted up the serpent in the wilderness, even so must the Son of Man be lifted up, ¹⁵ that whoever believes in Him should not perish but have eternal life. ¹⁶ For God so loved the world that He gave His only begotten Son, that whoever believes in Him should not perish but have everlasting life. ¹⁷ For God did not send His Son into the world to condemn the world, but that the world through Him might be saved. ¹⁸ "He who believes in Him is not condemned; but he who does not believe is condemned already, because he has not believed in the name of the only begotten Son of God. ¹⁹ And this is the condemnation, that the light has come into the world, and men loved darkness rather than light, because their deeds were evil. ²⁰ For everyone practicing evil hates the light and does not come to the light, lest his deeds should be exposed. ²¹ But he who does the truth comes to the light, that his deeds may be clearly seen, that they have been done in God."

* Original Artwork by Antonio Collins

Numbers 21:7-9

Therefore the people came to Moses, and said, "We have sinned, for we have spoken against the LORD and against you; pray to the LORD that He take away the serpents from us." So Moses prayed for the people. ⁸Then the Lord said to Moses, "Make a fiery *serpent,* and set it on a pole; and it shall be that everyone who is bitten, when he looks at it, shall live." ⁹ So Moses made a bronze serpent, and put it on a pole; and so it was, if a serpent had bitten anyone, when he looked at the bronze serpent, he lived.

Mark 9:24 Immediately the father of the child cried out and said with tears, "Lord, I believe; help my unbelief!"

John 11:40 Jesus said to her, "Did I not say to you that if you would believe you would see the glory of God?"

Meditation Points:

1. All people are candidates for salvation. There is nothing that can disqualify a person.
2. We become a believer when we believe in our heart and confess with our mouth that Jesus is Lord.
3. With belief comes visible change. **Change is not change until we change.** When a person genuinely believes something, action will follow. For example, if a person believes a million dollars is buried in their front yard, they will start digging. Belief is followed by action.
4. It is possible to believe, yet have unbelief. We must believe that *God is* and He answers when we call.
5. Ask God for help.

Prayer of Salvation:

Dear Heavenly Father,

I believe that Jesus Christ died on the cross and His Blood was shed for the forgiveness of my sin and the healing of my body, mind, and emotions. I repent of sin. Teach Me Your ways, O Lord. Let my eyes be open to see the vision You sent me to the earth to fulfill. Let my ears be open to hear Your still small voice. My hands must prosper in all they do. I am Your child and Your representative. I yield my destiny to You and renounce every demonic tie - known and unknown. I am filled with the Power of the Holy Spirit. I am Your beloved child. In Christ, I will never be ashamed.

In Jesus Name, Amen

Journal Prompt:

God did not take the serpents away as the people *asked* in Numbers 21. But God did make a way of healing, deliverance, & freedom, in-spite-of their circumstances. Those who made a quality decision to turn from looking at the problem to the Solution *lived.* Identify toxic areas in your life that you must turn from and positive alternatives to turn to. Write about it.

_____
_____
_____
_____
_____
_____
_____
_____
_____
_____
_____
_____
_____
_____
_____
_____
_____
_____
_____
_____

Jeremiah 29:11-13

For I know the thoughts that I think toward you, says the Lord, thoughts of peace and not of evil, to give you a future and a hope. [12] Then you will call upon Me and go and pray to Me, and I will listen to you. [13] And you will seek Me and find *Me,* when you search for Me with all your heart.

Session 2: The Authorization

Genesis 1:26-28

Then God said, "Let Us make man in Our image, according to Our likeness; let them have dominion over the fish of the sea, over the birds of the air, and over the cattle, over all the earth and over every creeping thing that creeps on the earth." ^{27} So God created man in His *own* image; in the image of God He created him; male and female He created them. ^{28} Then God blessed them, and God said to them, "Be fruitful and multiply; fill the earth and subdue it; have dominion over the fish of the sea, over the birds of the air, and over every living thing that moves on the earth."

Matthew 20:28

just as the Son of Man did not come to be served, but to serve, and to give His life a ransom for many."

Romans 6:14-23

For sin shall not have dominion over you, for you are not under law but under grace.

From Slaves of Sin to Slaves of God

^{15} What then? Shall we sin because we are not under law but under grace? Certainly not! ^{16} Do you not know that to whom you present yourselves slaves to obey, you are that one's slaves whom you obey, whether of sin *leading* to death, or of obedience *leading* to righteousness? ^{17} But God be thanked that *though* you were slaves of sin, yet you obeyed from the heart that form of doctrine to which you were delivered. ^{18} And having been set free from sin, you became slaves of righteousness. ^{19} I speak in human *terms* because of the weakness of your flesh. For just as you presented your members *as* slaves of uncleanness, and of lawlessness *leading* to *more* lawlessness, so now present your members *as* slaves *of* righteousness for holiness. ^{20} For when you were slaves of sin, you were free in regard to righteousness. ^{21} What fruit did you have then in the things of which you are now ashamed? For the end of those things *is* death. ^{22} But now having been set free from sin, and having become slaves of God, you have your fruit to holiness, and the end, everlasting life. ^{23} For the wages of sin *is* death, but the gift of God *is* eternal life in Christ Jesus our Lord.

Genesis 4:6-7

So the LORD said to Cain, "Why are you angry? And why has your countenance fallen? ^{7} If you do well, will you not be accepted? And if you do not do well, sin lies at the door. And its desire *is* for you, but you should rule over it."

Ephesians 2:10

For we are His workmanship, created in Christ Jesus for good works, which God prepared beforehand that we should walk in them.

Psalm 100

Make a joyful shout to the LORD, all you lands!
^{2} Serve the LORD with gladness;
Come before His presence with singing.
^{3} Know that the LORD, He *is* God;
It is He *who* has made us, and not we ourselves;
We are His people and the sheep of His pasture.
^{4} Enter into His gates with thanksgiving,
And into His courts with praise.
Be thankful to Him, *and* bless His name.
^{5} For the LORD *is* good;
His mercy *is* everlasting,
And His truth *endures* to all generations.

Meditation Points:

1. We, all people, were created in the image of God and have been given dominion power.

2. Sin is missing the mark. Imagine a target with a bullseye in the center. Sin is *everything* outside of the bullseye. Jesus Christ came into the world and gave His life as a ransom for many. Amnesty has been granted from the stronghold of sin. Nonetheless, people remain bound to the destiny hijacker – satan – and his legion of demonic oppression. Why the none-the-less portion?

3. God desires your success, even more than you do. **John 17:22-23** reminds us, "And the glory which You gave Me I have given them, that they may be one just as We are one: [23] I in them, and You in Me; that they may be made perfect in one, and that the world may know that You have sent Me, and have loved them as You have loved Me."

Journal Prompt:

Identify personal areas of your life where / when you have settled for a none-the-less portion. What is your exit plan to move forward?

___

Romans 3:21-26

[21] But now the righteousness of God apart from the law is revealed, being witnessed by the Law and the Prophets, [22] even the righteousness of God, through faith in Jesus Christ, to all and on all who believe. For there is no difference; [23] for all have sinned and fall short of the glory of God, [24] being justified freely by His grace through the redemption that is in Christ Jesus, [25] whom God set forth *as* a propitiation by His blood, through faith, to demonstrate His righteousness, because in His forbearance God had passed over the sins that were previously committed, [26] to demonstrate at the present time His righteousness, that He might be just and the justifier of the one who has faith in Jesus.

Session 3: The Authority

Ephesians 1:3-14

Blessed *be* the God and Father of our Lord Jesus Christ, who has blessed us with every spiritual blessing in the heavenly *places* in Christ, [4] just as He chose us in Him before the foundation of the world, that we should be holy and without blame before Him in love, [5] having predestined us to adoption as sons by Jesus Christ to Himself, according to the good pleasure of His will, [6] to the praise of the glory of His grace, by which He made us accepted in the Beloved. [7] In Him we have redemption through His blood, the forgiveness of sins, according to the riches of His grace [8] which He made to abound toward us in all wisdom and prudence, [9] having made known to us the mystery of His will, according to His good pleasure which He purposed in Himself, [10] that in the dispensation of the fullness of the times He might gather together in one all things in Christ, both which are in heaven and which are on earth—in Him. [11] In Him also we have obtained an inheritance, being predestined according to the purpose of Him who works all things according to the counsel of His will, [12] that we who first trusted in Christ should be to the praise of His glory. [13] In Him you also *trusted*, after you heard the word of truth, the gospel of your salvation; in whom also, having believed, you were sealed with the Holy Spirit of promise, [14] who is the guarantee of our inheritance until the redemption of the purchased possession, to the praise of His glory.

Matthew 28:18-20

And Jesus came and spoke to them, saying, "All authority has been given to Me in heaven and on earth. [19] Go therefore and make disciples of all the nations, baptizing them in the name of the Father and of the Son and of the Holy Spirit, [20] teaching them to observe all things that I have commanded you; and lo, I am with you always, *even* to the end of the age." Amen.

[C]asting down arguments and every high thing that exalts itself against the knowledge of God, bringing every thought into captivity to the obedience of Christ, and being ready to punish all disobedience when your obedience is fulfilled.
2 Corinthians 10:5-6

The enemy works to deposit contraceptives into the powerful womb of the mind so Godly seeds do not conceive. To cast down arguments and every high thing that exalts itself against the knowledge of God means to evict negative and destructive imaginations that arise to cause confusion, insecurity, anxiety, clouded thinking, and every other terror. Every thought must be brought into captivity to the obedience of Christ by purposely directing meditations of the mind and confessions of the mouth, which become the condition of the heart.

Only refusing to think about something leaves vast open space in the mind for even worse thoughts to swarm. Seeds of the Word must be sown in the mind. As the Word of God firmly roots, it establishes dominion. The mind transforms into an arsenal ready to punish all disobedience when obedience has been fulfilled.

*Exert from *The Robe of Many Colors*, by Diana Robinson

Colossians 2:13-15

And you, being dead in your trespasses and the uncircumcision of your flesh, He has made alive together with Him, having forgiven you all trespasses, [14] having wiped out the handwriting of requirements that was against us, which was contrary to us. And He has taken it out of the way, having nailed it to the cross. [15] Having disarmed principalities and powers, He made a public spectacle of them, triumphing over them in it.

Meditation Points:

1. You are already blessed.
2. You were chosen before the foundation of the world.
3. You are without blame before God through Jesus Christ.
4. You are not a candidate for shame nor a victim of low-self esteem. Your identity is in Christ Jesus.
5. You are not a bastard. You have been adopted into the family of God according to the good pleasure of His will.
6. You are accepted in the Beloved.
7. You have been redeemed from sin and the consequence thereof, through the Blood of Jesus.
8. You are a recipient of Grace.
9. You operate in wisdom from above. The mystery of His will is revealed to you.
10. You are a beneficiary of the inheritance. There is an earthly distribution, as well as, a heavenly distribution.
11. You serve a trustworthy God, who is worthy to be praised.
12. You are a partaker of the gospel (exceedingly good news will always be your testimony).
13. You are sealed with the Holy Spirit of Promise.
14. You practice the principles of God, therefore you are guaranteed good success.

Journal Prompt:

1 Corinthians 16:9
For a great and effective door has opened to me, and *there are* many adversaries.

You have all the authority you need to access every door of opportunity set before you. You will triumph & prevail over any adversity opposing your entry.

What thoughts do you need to cast down and replace to move forward?

_____
_____
_____
_____
_____
_____
_____
_____
_____
_____
_____
_____
_____
_____
_____
_____
_____
_____
_____
_____
_____
_____
_____
_____
_____

Session 4: The Power

> **Deuteronomy 8:18**
>
> "And you shall remember the Lord your God, for *it is* He who gives you power to get wealth, that He may establish His covenant which He swore to your fathers, as *it is* this day.

> **Ephesians 3:20-21**
>
> Now to Him who is able to do exceedingly abundantly above all that we ask or think, according to the power that works in us, ²¹ to Him *be* glory in the church by Christ Jesus to all generations, forever and ever. Amen.

> **Hebrews 11:3**
>
> By faith we understand that the worlds were framed by the word of God, so that the things which are seen were not made of things which are visible.

Therefore do not cast away your confidence, which has great reward. For you have need of endurance, so that after you have done the will of God, you may receive the promise: "For yet a little while, *And* He who is coming will come and will not tarry. Now the just shall live by faith; But if *anyone* draws back, My soul has no pleasure in him."

Hebrews 10:35-38

We cannot cast away our confidence; we need it to endure to the point of receiving the promise. The casting away of confidence is cunning and appears as:

- Believing God for everyone else's situation, except your own.
- Giving quality insightful advice to everyone else, except yourself.
- Performing with excellence at work, in church, and in the community; making everyone else look good, then returning home depleted and frustrated.

In fear, even the thought of failure brings condemnation and causes one to draw back. In confidence, there is no failure; only opportunity to perfect and spring forward. The *just* shall live by faith. The *just* are born-again believers, justified by the Blood of Jesus Christ. Because of the Blood, every spirit of destruction and untimely death working against the manifestation of the vision must pass over.

With vision, comes two types of provision. Provision to *do* the vision and provision generated *from* the completed work. God has so much He wants to get to us. Establishment of the vision creates an inlet so the immeasurable wealth of God can flow to us. When we reject carrying out the vision, we are rejecting God and His provision for us.

*Exert from *The Robe of Many Colors*, by Diana Robinson

> **John 14:12-18**
>
> "Most assuredly, I say to you, he who believes in Me, the works that I do he will do also; and greater *works* than these he will do, because I go to My Father. ¹³ And whatever you ask in My name, that I will do, that the Father may be glorified in the Son. ¹⁴ If you ask anything in My name, I will do *it.*
>
> **Jesus Promises Another Helper**
>
> ¹⁵ "If you love Me, keep My commandments. ¹⁶ And I will pray the Father, and He will give you another Helper, that He may abide with you forever— ¹⁷ the Spirit of truth, whom the world cannot receive, because it neither sees Him nor knows Him; but you know Him, for He dwells with you and will be in you. ¹⁸ I will not leave you orphans; I will come to you.

Meditation Points:

1. You can do all things through Christ who strengthens you.
2. You have the power to do all things with excellence as unto the Lord. **Isaiah 40:10** Behold, the Lord God shall come with a strong *hand,* And His arm shall rule for Him; Behold, His reward *is* with Him, And His work before Him.
3. The work of your hands must proper. **Isaiah 3:10** "Say to the righteous that *it shall be* well *with them,* For they shall eat the fruit of their doings.

Philippians 4:13

I can do all things through Christ who strengthens me.

Colossians 3:23-24

And whatever you do, do it heartily, as to the Lord and not to men, ^{24} knowing that from the Lord you will receive the reward of the inheritance; for you serve the Lord Christ.

Proverbs 19:18

A man's gift makes room for him, And brings him before great men.

Proverbs 22:29

Do you see a man *who* excels in his work? He will stand before kings; He will not stand before unknown *men.*

Proverbs 3:25-26

Do not be afraid of sudden terror, Nor of trouble from the wicked when it comes; ^{26} For the LORD will be your confidence, And will keep your foot from being caught.

Journal Prompt:

1 John 4:4

You are of God, little children, and have overcome them, because He who is in you is greater than he who is in the world.

The Power of the Holy Spirit worketh in you and through you.
You are anointed for great exploits.

Intentionally focus on building confidence in a specific area of your life where it is lacking. What will you say & do?

Session 5: The Planting

> **Isaiah 51:16**
>
> And I have put My words in your mouth; I have covered you with the shadow of My hand, That I may plant the heavens, Lay the foundations of the earth, And say to Zion 'You *are* My people.'"

Vision is from God for us. Manifestation is through us for God. Before we were formed in our mother's womb, all our days were already written. The vision was first. Then the person was hand-crafted and named to fulfill the vision by the Creator. Our inward parts were fashioned and molded with all things required to manifest the vision. People were not created and then vision assigned or passed out. Confirmation of this is found in Psalm 139:16, "Your eyes saw my substance, being yet unformed. And in Your book they all were written, The days fashioned for me, When as yet there were none of them."

Exert from The Robe of Many Colors, by Diana Robinson

> **Psalm 107:20**
>
> He sent His word and healed them, And delivered *them* from their destructions.

> **Matthew 6:10**
>
> Your kingdom come. Your will be done On earth as *it is* in heaven.

> **Job 22:28**
>
> You will also declare a thing, And it will be established for you; So light will shine on your ways.

> **Proverbs 18:21**
>
> Death and life *are* in the power of the tongue, And those who love it will eat its fruit.

> **Matthew 8:5-13 (MSG)**
>
> [5-6] As Jesus entered the village of Capernaum, a Roman captain came up in a panic and said, "Master, my servant is sick. He can't walk. He's in terrible pain." [7] Jesus said, "I'll come and heal him." [8-9] "Oh, no," said the captain. "I don't want to put you to all that trouble. Just give the order and my servant will be fine. I'm a man who takes orders and gives orders. I tell one soldier, 'Go,' and he goes; to another, 'Come,' and he comes; to my slave, 'Do this,' and he does it." [10-12] Taken aback, Jesus said, "I've yet to come across this kind of simple trust in Israel, the very people who are supposed to know all about God and how he works. This man is the vanguard of many outsiders who will soon be coming from all directions—streaming in from the east, pouring in from the west, sitting down at God's kingdom banquet alongside Abraham, Isaac, and Jacob. Then those who grew up 'in the faith' but had no faith will find themselves out in the cold, outsiders to grace and wondering what happened." [13] Then Jesus turned to the captain and said, "Go. What you believed could happen has happened." At that moment his servant became well.

> **Ezekiel 36:33-36**
>
> 'Thus says the Lord GOD: "On the day that I cleanse you from all your iniquities, I will also enable *you* to dwell in the cities, and the ruins shall be rebuilt. [34] The desolate land shall be tilled instead of lying desolate in the sight of all who pass by. [35] So they will say, 'This land that was desolate has become like the garden of Eden; and the wasted, desolate, and ruined cities *are now* fortified *and* inhabited.' [36] Then the nations which are left all around you shall know that I, the LORD, have rebuilt the ruined places *and* planted what was desolate. I, the LORD, have spoken *it,* and I will do *it.*"

Meditation Points:

1. The Word of God is true—AND it is true unto you.
2. The Blood of Jesus cleanses your conscience from dead works in order for you to serve the Living God. (*see* Hebrews 9:14)
3. The Glory of God has risen upon you for great exploits. **Isaiah 60:1** Arise, shine; For your light has come! And the glory of the Lord is risen upon you.
4. You are an ambassador for Christ Jesus. People are watching and being influenced by your life. **2 Corinthians 5:20** Now then, we are ambassadors for Christ, as though God were pleading through us: we implore *you* on Christ's behalf, be reconciled to God.
5. You are distinctly and uniquely made to fulfill a specific assignment in the earth. No one else can do it.
6. You are Graced for every life position you hold: parent, grandparent, sibling, employer, employee, co-worker, neighbor, care-giver, etc. You are irreplaceable!
7. There is no problem that God has not already provided the solution for. **1 Corinthians 10:13** No temptation has overtaken you except such as is common to man; but God *is* faithful, who will not allow you to be tempted beyond what you are able, but with the temptation will also make the way of escape, that you may be able to bear *it*.

Journal Prompt:

Luke 8:11
"Now the parable is this:
The seed is the word of God.

Every word spoken, is a seed sowed. You shall have what-so-ever you say. Watch your mouth!

Psalm 141:3
Set a guard, O Lord, over my mouth; Keep watch over the door of my lips.

List & Declare
Personal POSITIVE Affirmations:

_____
_____
_____
_____
_____
_____
_____
_____
_____
_____
_____
_____
_____
_____
_____
_____
_____
_____
_____
_____
_____
_____
_____

Session 6: The Fruition

James 1:21-25

Therefore lay aside all filthiness and overflow of wickedness, and receive with meekness the implanted word, which is able to save your souls. ²² But be doers of the word, and not hearers only, deceiving yourselves. ²³ For if anyone is a hearer of the word and not a doer, he is like a man observing his natural face in a mirror; ²⁴ for he observes himself, goes away, and immediately forgets what kind of man he was. ²⁵ But he who looks into the perfect law of liberty and continues *in it,* and is not a forgetful hearer but a doer of the work, this one will be blessed in what he does.

Romans 11:29

For the gifts and the calling of God *are* irrevocable.

For *there is* no sorcery against Jacob, Nor any divination against Israel. It now must be said of Jacob And of Israel, 'Oh, what God has done!'

Numbers 23:23

Henceforth, there is no sorcery against the old you (Jacob); nor any divination against the new you (Israel), that can void the vision God sent you into this earth to manifest. The witnesses; even the whispers, whiners, and wonderers, will be moved to declare, "Oh, what God has done!"

Perform the Word

On this earth we have one life to live. People are looking for answers. A Christian's response during tribulations testifies to the power of Christ. Triumphing in tragedy by standing firmly on the Word of God and acting on His principles leaves a permanent impression with others. Performing the word makes the invisible visible.

By faith, we have the ability to *see* in the invisible realm and retrieve the blueprint for visible manifestation. The Lord said to Jeremiah, in Jeremiah 1:12, "You have seen well, for I am ready to perform My word." When the Angel announced to Mary that she was the chosen mother of Jesus, she grasped the seed needed for conception within her womb from the invisible realm. Her confession gave consent in Luke 1:38, "Behold the maidservant of the Lord! Let it be to me according to your word."

*Exert from The Robe of Many Colors, by Diana Robinson

Deuteronomy 28:1-8

"Now it shall come to pass, if you diligently obey the voice of the Lord your God, to observe carefully all His commandments which I command you today, that the Lord your God will set you high above all nations of the earth. ² And all these blessings shall come upon you and overtake you, because you obey the voice of the Lord your God:

³ "Blessed *shall* you *be* in the city, and blessed *shall* you *be* in the country.

⁴ "Blessed *shall be* the fruit of your body, the produce of your ground and the increase of your herds, the increase of your cattle and the offspring of your flocks.

⁵ "Blessed *shall be* your basket and your kneading bowl.

⁶ "Blessed *shall* you *be* when you come in, and blessed *shall* you *be* when you go out.

⁷ "The Lord will cause your enemies who rise against you to be defeated before your face; they shall come out against you one way and flee before you seven ways.

⁸ "The Lord will command the blessing on you in your storehouses and in all to which you set your hand, and He will bless you in the land which the Lord your God is giving you.

Meditation Points:

1. What God has for you, is for you. No imposter can take it and no place-holder can remain in your reserved position.
2. Preparation + Opportunity = Success
3. What you are doing when no one is looking, determines your level when you come into view.
4. Your level of obedience and your level of sacrifice, determine your level of elevation.
5. Obedience Overcomes Obstacles
6. As you do the *possible*, God will do the *impossible*.
7. Core Values for Elevation: Faith, Understanding, & Excellence

Luke 6:44
For every tree is known by its own fruit. For *men* do not gather figs from thorns, nor do they gather grapes from a bramble bush.

Mark 10:27
But Jesus looked at them and said, "With men *it is* impossible, but not with God; for with God all things are possible."

Hebrews 11:6
But without faith *it is* impossible to please *Him,* for he who comes to God must believe that He is, and *that* He is a rewarder of those who diligently seek Him.

Journal Prompt:

2 Corinthians 8:12
For if there is first a willing mind, *it is* accepted according to what one has, *and* not according to what he does not have.

God does not expect you to do anything with something He has not given you; but He does expect you to do everything with what He has given you.

Start at the level you are at. Build and advance from there. What is your action plan?

_____
_____
_____
_____
_____
_____
_____
_____
_____
_____
_____
_____
_____
_____
_____
_____
_____
_____
_____
_____
_____
_____

Journal Pages
w/ Inspirational Scriptures

Write Unto the Lord

Ezekiel 36:26

I will give you a new heart and put a new spirit within you; I will take the heart of stone out of your flesh and give you a heart of flesh.

Romans 12:21

Do not be overcome by evil, but overcome evil with good.

Revelation 12:11

And they overcame him by the blood of the Lamb and by the word of their testimony, and they did not love their lives to the death.

James 1:4

But let patience have *its* perfect work,
that you may be perfect and complete, lacking nothing.

James 1:5

If any of you lacks wisdom, let him ask of God, who gives to all liberally and without reproach, and it will be given to him.

James 1:6

But let him ask in faith, with no doubting, for he who doubts is like a wave of the sea driven and tossed by the wind.

James 1:17

Every good gift and every perfect gift is from above, and comes down from the Father of lights, with whom there is no variation or shadow of turning.

James 1:22
But be doers of the word, and not hearers only, deceiving yourselves.

James 1:25

But he who looks into the perfect law of liberty and continues *in it,* and is not a forgetful hearer but a doer of the work, this one will be blessed in what he does.

James 4:7
Therefore submit to God. Resist the devil and he will flee from you.

James 4:8

Draw near to God and He will draw near to you. Cleanse *your* hands, *you* sinners; and purify *your* hearts, *you* double-minded.

John 14:6

Jesus said to him, "I am the way, the truth, and the life.
No one comes to the Father except through Me."

John 14:11

"Believe Me that I *am* in the Father and the Father in Me, or else believe Me for the sake of the works themselves."

John 14:12

"Most assuredly, I say to you, he who believes in Me, the works that I do he will do also; and greater *works* than these he will do, because I go to My Father."

John 14:15

"If you love Me, keep My commandments."

John 14:16

"And I will pray the Father, and He will give you another Helper, that He may abide with you forever—"

John 14:18
"I will not leave you orphans; I will come to you."

John 14:26

"But the Helper, the Holy Spirit, whom the Father will send in My name, He will teach you all things, and bring to your remembrance all things that I said to you."

John 14:27

"Peace I leave with you, My peace I give to you; not as the world gives do I give to you. Let not your heart be troubled, neither let it be afraid."

Ephesians 1:3

Blessed *be* the God and Father of our Lord Jesus Christ, who has blessed us with every spiritual blessing in the heavenly *places* in Christ,

Ephesians 1:4

just as He chose us in Him before the foundation of the world, that we should be holy and without blame before Him in love,

Ephesians 1:5

having predestined us to adoption as sons by Jesus Christ to Himself, according to the good pleasure of His will,

Ephesians 1:6

to the praise of the glory of His grace,
by which He made us accepted in the Beloved.

Ephesians 1:7

In Him we have redemption through His blood,
the forgiveness of sins, according to the riches of His grace

Ephesians 1:18

the eyes of your understanding being enlightened; that you may know what is the hope of His calling, what are the riches of the glory of His inheritance in the saints,

Ephesians 3:16

that He would grant you, according to the riches of His glory,
to be strengthened with might through His Spirit in the inner man,

Ephesians 3:17

that Christ may dwell in your hearts through faith; that you,
being rooted and grounded in love,

Ephesians 3:18

may be able to comprehend with all the saints
what *is* the width and length and depth and height—

Ephesians 3:19

to know the love of Christ which passes knowledge;
that you may be filled with all the fullness of God.

Ephesians 3:20

Now to Him who is able to do exceedingly abundantly above all that we ask or think, according to the power that works in us,

Deuteronomy 28:12

The Lord will open to you His good treasure, the heavens, to give the rain to your land in its season, and to bless all the work of your hand.
You shall lend to many nations, but you shall not borrow.

Isaiah 54:17

No weapon formed against you shall prosper, And every tongue *which* rises against you in judgment You shall condemn. This *is* the heritage of the servants of the Lord, And their righteousness *is* from Me," Says the Lord.

Haggai 2:23

'In that day,' says the Lord of hosts, 'I will take you, Zerubbabel My servant, the son of Shealtiel,' says the Lord, 'and will make you like a signet *ring;* for I have chosen you,' says the Lord of hosts."

Zechariah 2:8

For thus says the Lord of hosts: "He sent Me after glory, to the nations which plunder you; for he who touches you touches the apple of His eye.

Psalm 139:16

Your eyes saw my substance, being yet unformed. And in Your book they all were written, The days fashioned for me, When *as yet there were* none of them.

Psalm 139:17

How precious also are Your thoughts to me, O God!
How great is the sum of them!

Proverbs 18:16
A man's gift makes room for him, And brings him before great men.

Proverbs 22:29

Do you see a man *who* excels in his work?
He will stand before kings; He will not stand before unknown *men*.

OBEDIENCE
OVERCOMES
OBSTACLES